C000093977

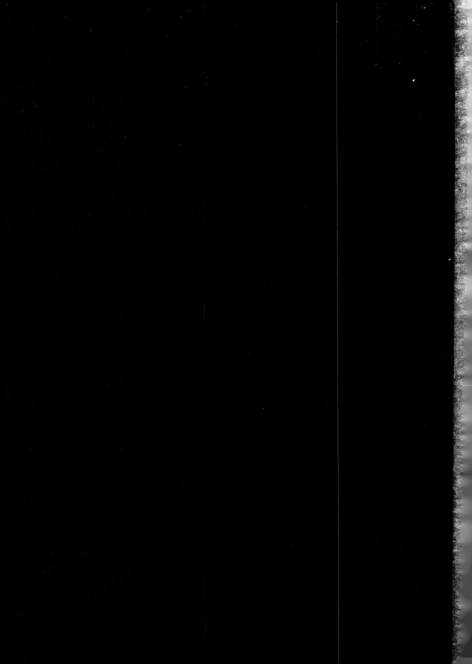

A clay model for the bronze sculpture
of Laurie Lee by Lyn Bamber

LAURIE LEE

a many-coated man

With contributions by Rt Hon. David Blunkett, MP
Canon William Brassell · Dr Christopher Fry
P. J. Kavanagh · Bobby Kok
Tony Lacey · Roger McGough
John Mortimer · Brian Patten
His Excellency Richard Ryan,
the Ambassador of Ireland to Spain

❧

Edited by Jock Gallagher

VIKING

VIKING

Published by the Penguin Group
Penguin Books Ltd, 27 Wrights Lane, London w8 5tz, England
Penguin Putnam Inc., 375 Hudson Street, New York, New York 10014, USA
Penguin Books Australia Ltd, Ringwood, Victoria, Australia
Penguin Books Canada Ltd, 10 Alcorn Avenue, Toronto, Ontario, Canada m4v 3b2
Penguin Books (NZ) Ltd, 182–190 Wairau Road, Auckland 10, New Zealand

Penguin Books Ltd, Registered Offices: Harmondsworth, Middlesex, England

First published 1998
1 3 5 7 9 10 8 6 4 2

Introduction and editorial matter copyright © Jock Gallagher, 1998
John Mortimer's speech copyright © Advanpress Ltd, 1998
All other speeches copyright © the individual speakers, 1998

Set in 10½/14½ pt Monotype Baskerville by
Rowland Phototypesetting Ltd, Bury St Edmunds, Suffolk
Printed in England by Clays Ltd, St Ives plc
A CIP catalogue record for this book is available from the British Library

ISBN 0 670 8871708

CONTENTS

List of Illustrations ix

Introduction xiii

Canon William Brassell 1

Christopher Fry 4

John Mortimer 12

Roger McGough 19

Bobby Kok 27

Tony Lacey 32

His Excellency Richard Ryan 41

Brian Patten 52

Rt Hon. David Blunkett, MP 58

P. J. Kavanagh 67

LIST OF ILLUSTRATIONS

A clay model for the bronze sculpture
of Laurie Lee by Lyn Bamber   iii
(© Lyn Bamber)

Laurie as a child   xi

Laurie as a young man   7

Laurie with guitar   17
(© *Evening Standard*)

Laurie entertaining Cathy and Jessy   29

Ladies' man and wit   37
(© Bryan Wharton)

Laurie in the Woolpack   49
(© *Mail on Sunday*)

Country gentleman   57

Laurie with the Rt. Hon.
David Blunkett, MP   63

The churchyard at Slad   71

Laurie, at a carefree, coatless age. He didn't know it at the time, but his innocent inquisitiveness was already filling his mind with vivid pictures that he would magically recapture in his writing. It was his arrival in Slad, at the age of three, that provided him with the opening of *Cider with Rosie*.

I was set down from the carrier's cart . . . and there with a sense of bewilderment and terror my life in the village began.

Later, Laurie marvelled at the interest in reading instilled in him by his mother and described himself as part of 'our country's first literate peasantry'.

INTRODUCTION

On the morning his friends and admirers gathered to celebrate the long and creative life of Laurie Lee, the sun emerged from the dark autumn clouds to shine with unexpected brilliance. It was as if Nature was making amends for the day of his funeral, in May, when the rain had lashed mourners at the cold, hillside graveyard in Laurie's beloved Slad Valley in Gloucestershire.

The congregation, filing into St James's Church in London's Piccadilly, accepted the apology with deep gratitude and, although all the tributes were moving and some of them particularly poignant, there was barely a hint of sadness in the ecclesiastical air.

Laurie would have understood and he would undoubtedly have enjoyed the occasion enormously. The literati and the glitterati had joined forces, come out in their finery, to pay their respects and acknowledge their affection for a much-loved writer, poet, musician and irrepressible wit.

The two days were as different as only English days can be and yet both seem, particularly in retrospect, to be gloriously appropriate.

In the immediate aftermath of his death, the emotions aroused among many of Laurie's friends were a cruel mix of sadness, anger and bewilderment. By his own recognition, he had long been 'not very well' but the wheeziness, the failing eyesight, the aches, the pains and the gentle frailty had been resolutely absorbed into his demeanour and, if anything, seemed to reinforce his air of indestructibility.

Lesser mortals might have succumbed to any one of his ailments but Laurie turned each of them into a mere talking point, as relevant only as the weather. As I am sure he intended, his friends, too, shrugged them off and, instead, continued to revel in the vigour of his intellect and the embracing warmth of his razor-sharp wit.

So, on that black morning when he was laid to rest – in what he described as the 'deep, green, juicy, damp valley seemingly always lashed by Welsh rain' – we were still shocked by the final suddenness of his loss. He had played so many different roles in our various lives, each of them too important to be laid aside with anything less than a heavy heart. Some of us subconsciously took the edge off our grief by giving vent to another powerful emotion – anger.

Much of my personal angst, it must be said, was born out of guilt: I had been planning to drop in to see him for several weeks and had put it off once too often. Suddenly it was too late. For no good reason, he was snatched from us – with so many things left unsaid and so many things left undone.

In the interceding months, the anger subsided, to be

replaced by the unexpected joy of remembrance. The mind accepted he had gone and with that came the confirmation he was irreplaceable. The defence mechanisms kicked in and one realized that the next best thing to the effervescence of Laurie's conversation were the myriad memories so easily evoked.

We therefore arrived at St James's lifted by the brightness of the late autumn sunshine and bathed in the warmth of our personal recollections.

❦

My first meeting with Laurie was cool, almost to the point of hostility.

Or so I thought.

It was in autumn 1967, and I had ventured forth from the BBC studios in Birmingham to try to persuade him to do some broadcasting.

Safe in his Cotswold stronghold, he was resolute in his resistance. I got the distinct impression he was not particularly enamoured of a BBC crass enough to employ a Clydeside Scot to make programmes about rural England.

No, he didn't want to be on the wireless, and *No*, he couldn't be persuaded by any amount of flattery.

I had tried hard: I dropped a mention of an article (which subsequently appeared in *I Can't Stay Long*) on writing autobiography that he'd had published in the book section of *The New York Times*. I thought quoting from it would stand me in good stead and so I told him my favourite line was: 'For me it is a celebration of living and an attempt to hoard its sensations.'

'Hmmn,' he said. 'It is rather good, isn't it.' But he still declined my invitation.

So I tried again. I told him my wife was a great fan of his poetry and one of her most treasured possessions was an auto-graphed and much-thumbed copy of *My Many-Coated Man*.

'Hmmn,' he said. 'She's obviously a very discerning lady.'

But it didn't work. Nor did any of my other soft-soap tech-niques. He remained stubborn.

Or so I thought.

I accepted defeat and, crestfallen at my failure, I rose to leave.

'Haven't you got any more flattery, then?' he asked and, for the first time, I saw the twinkle that was to become so familiar down the years. 'You could always try money,' he grinned.

It was a great performance and it worked. In my enthusias-tic rush to clinch a deal, I found myself instantly doubling my intended offer.

The ensuing programme – about the contemporary Cotswolds – was the first of many we made together, but it was not the last time he rebuffed my initial overtures.

However, I did learn to handle negotiations on behalf of the BBC a little better. Instead of *always* increasing the offer, occa-sionally (when my budgets were particularly stretched) I said I would have to settle for someone else reading his poetry.

'Who?' he would ask. I always named the same dreary actor

and Laurie always demanded: 'Why him? He murders the language.'

My answer was inevitably: 'He's all we can afford on the budget, Laurie.'

'Damn you! I'd rather do it myself for nothing,' he insisted, although, of course, we both knew it wouldn't come to that.

While he made haggling over fees into an art form and revelled in his reputation as a tough negotiator (causing considerable anguish to several publishers and television producers), Laurie had a personal generosity second to none. Not once in hundreds of sessions at the Chelsea Arts Club was I allowed to buy a drink – 'Member's privilege, old chap' – and I could pay restaurant bills only when I said I would be getting it back on my BBC expenses.

Then, when I was involved in the launch of an arts festival in the small Worcestershire town where I live, Laurie immediately agreed to take part and was offended when I said we would be able to offer only a meagre fee. 'I don't take money from my friends,' he said. 'If you want me, you'll have to take me for nothing.'

It was, however, never wise to push your luck with Laurie, as I found to my cost when, some years later, I invited him to make a second appearance at the festival. He again agreed, warmly and generously, to come to read some of his poetry and a few excerpts from his books.

But just a couple of days before the event, he said he wasn't feeling well and besides, 'I don't have a decent pair of shoes.' It was an excuse distinctly reminiscent of his I-haven't-got-a-coat reason for giving *Cider with Rosie* to the Hogarth Press rather than to André Deutsch.

My blood ran cold.

I was horrified and considerably embarrassed. Not only had I given him top billing for the festival but I had also persuaded Radio 4 to take the opportunity of recording the performance for *With Great Pleasure*, and Martin Jarvis and Jill Balcon were booked to do some of the readings.

However, with the anguish of Mr Deutsch very much in my mind and rather than harass Laurie with plaintive pleas to reconsider, I rushed around and eventually, on the morning of the event, persuaded Stephen Fry to be the replacement.

My relief lasted all of five minutes.

Just as I had tied up all the new arrangements, Laurie rang. 'I'm feeling very much better and Cathy and I are really looking forward to coming to the festival. When do you want us to arrive?'

Hurried telephone calls revealed that the BBC would record two editions of the programme, one with Laurie and the other with Stephen Fry.

Problem solved – or nearly.

When Laurie arrived and discovered the double booking, he was genuinely upset. 'You should have known I wouldn't let you down, dear boy.'

Then he proceeded to make me suffer for my lack of faith.

'You carry on with your friend, Stephen, and I'll get out of your hair. I'll go off and have a quiet drink,' he said with exceptional geniality.

The alarm bells rang. There are more than twenty pubs in our small town.

After a fruitless search of seventeen, I found Laurie in the eighteenth, just before 10 p.m.

It was not our most salubrious hostelry and a live band was apparently trying to get off the decibel-counter with its own brand of heavy metal.

Laurie wasn't drinking. 'Gosh, is it that late?' he inquired innocently. 'I've been enjoying the music so much I didn't notice the time.'

However, in a concession to my near-hysterical demeanour, he offered me reassurance: 'Don't worry, dear boy. They'll be just about ready for me now.'

I was not convinced, but he, of course, was right.

Late as it was, he was given a standing ovation – just for walking into the hall. And such was his magic, he was still signing copies of his book and chatting to enthusiastic admirers at midnight!

Many stories about Laurie border on the legendary.

Was *Cider with Rosie* really only a success because it was published at the end of a long printers' strike, as he often suggested?

Did he really meet two schoolgirls in Slad, who had come looking for his grave?

Did he really loiter in bookshops making sure his books were well displayed?

The twinkle in his eye when he recounted these sort of tales didn't help one to make a reasoned judgement. It could have been an indication that he was reliving fond memories, or that he was indulging in one of his favourite occupations – building up the Lee folklore.

That was clearly a family trait he learned at his mother's knee.

When my BBC colleague, Marjorie Lofthouse, interviewed his older step-sister Marjorie (for a Radio 4 programme I produced to mark the twenty-fifth anniversary of *Cider with Rosie*), she recalled the whole family sitting around the kitchen table listening to nightly stories from their mother, the redoubtable Nance. 'She wasn't a very good cook. She couldn't sew and she didn't much like housework, but she was very artistic and loved to tell us about her own childhood and teenage years in Gloucestershire.'

She also revealed how the family discovered Laurie had been secretly writing stories when he was still only about nine: 'The first one we found out about was *The Truth About The Browns* and it was very clever and amusing. It showed he had a very strong imagination, but it was such a private thing for Lol at that time and we didn't want to embarrass him by saying too much.'

The Browns were a Slad family later to feature in *Cider with Rosie* when the young Eileen Brown was his partner in duets at the annual parochial church tea. She was one of the girls most often suggested as the real-life Rosie but that, of course, is one of the secrets Laurie never revealed.

Nor did he ever lose his great predilection for privacy. One day, however, when he was in a particularly genial mood, he laid it aside, briefly, and showed me some photographs of his wife, Cathy, and daughter, Jessy.

They were stunning, and he was upset when I asked who had taken them. 'I did, of course,' he said almost crossly.

He wasn't too cross, however, to take up my suggestion that he put them together for a coffee-table book.

The exquisite *Two Women* was published in 1983 by André Deutsch and in the copy he gave me Laurie wrote: 'For Jock, who caused this to be done – and we love him in spite of it!'

That was a great moment but there was even better to come.

When *A Moment of War* was finally published in 1991, he gave me what he said was the first copy, hot off the press, and in it he wrote: 'To Jock – whose sturdy pressure helped me finish this book – con muchas gracias!'

And so it was, six months after his death, I found myself once again 'producing' a Laurie Lee special – his memorial service.

Cathy and Jessy had arranged the more formal aspects of the occasion with the Rector of St James's, the Reverend Donald Reeves, and had agreed the hymns and readings with Canon Bill Brassell, of Gloucester Cathedral, who had also officiated at the burial service in Slad.

For my part, I had a potential cast list that would have been the envy of the editor of any *Who's Who*. In the end, however, time constraints meant it was only possible to accommodate tributes from nine of Laurie's peers, friends and admirers: the Rt Hon. David Blunkett, MP, Dr Christopher Fry, P. J. Kavanagh, Bobby Kok, Tony Lacey, Roger McGough, John Mortimer, Brian Patten and His Excellency Richard Ryan, Irish Ambassador to Madrid.

But as befitted the church setting, it was Canon Brassell who set the scene for an extraordinary occasion.

Jock Gallagher

CANON WILLIAM BRASSELL

To open the batting at a memorial service for such a prestigious person as Laurie Lee – and in the presence of such an illustrious gathering of literary and musical talent – is a somewhat daunting task, especially for one whose acquaintance with Laurie and his family is comparatively recent compared with many of those present.

However, on the grounds that Jock said I should, that someone must and that Holy Writ suggests the last shall be first – note the order – I am happy, indeed privileged, to read a poem which is Laurie's tribute to the beauty of Gloucestershire's hills and valleys – described by P. J. Kavanagh, in his introduction to the *Collected Poems of Ivor Gurney*, as 'a landscape poised between the past and a dreamed of future, between history and paradise'.

In his poem, 'Field of Autumn', Laurie describes the paradise of the Slad Valley, in which he grew up; which he left but which he never forgot; and to which he subsequently returned to find his own paradise, with Cathy and Jessy and the green Cotswold Hills.

Slow moves the acid breath of noon
over the copper-coated hill,
slow from the wild crab's bearded breast
the palsied apples fall.

Like coloured smoke the day hangs fire,
taking the village without sound;
the vulture-headed sun lies low
chained to the violet ground.

The horse upon the rocky height
rolls all the valley in his eye,
but dares not raise his foot or move
his shoulder from the fly.

The sheep, snail-backed against the wall,
lifts her blind face but does not know
the cry her blackened tongue gives forth
is the first bleat of snow.

Each bird and stone, each roof and well,
feels the gold foot of autumn pass;
each spider binds with glittering snare
the splintered bones of grass.

Slow moves the hour that sucks our life,
slow drops the late wasp from the pear,
the rose tree's thread of scent draws thin –
and snaps upon the air.

⟐ Who are we to peer over the shoulder of greatness, to seek to fathom the depth and mystery of the writer, to try to capture the wild spirit of the poet in a form that won't reduce him to something ordinary?

Those of us with the difficult task of acknowledging the huge talents of Laurie Lee take heart from knowing that among this company – with each of you having your own cherished memory – his magic is forever powerful, forever secure, unshakeable even in my unsteady, uncertain hands.

It is, of course, to my *great advantage that Laurie lived among, and was much loved by, many of today's poets and writers, and some of them have come here to ensure that he is remembered in style.*

The first among equals, Dr Christopher Fry, a lifelong friend, a colleague in the Garrick Club and fellow poet. He, not unnaturally, chose to offer his tribute in verse.

CHRISTOPHER FRY

For Laurie Lee (1914–1997)

'Born I was to meet with Age,
And to walk life's pilgrimage' –
(That's Robert Herrick)
'But I'll spend my coming hours,
Drinking wine, and crowned with flowers' –
(Sang the Devon cleric)

'Far-fetched with tales of other worlds and ways,
My skin well-oiled with wines of the Levant' –
(That's Laurie Lee)
But how the Hell is one to celebrate
A life-long, life-imbibing celebrant? –
(That's simply me.)

Treading the grapes of time
He made that earth-engaging tipple
His vintage Slad.

Then with his music charmed the sun
Of Mexico, Tuscany and Spain
And Trinidad.

But still I find my eager feet
Return to Slad to attend the Whitsun Treat,
Standing to gawp at
The headlong charge of children and our Laurie
In triumph past the bullying Walt Kerry
Sprawled in a cow-pat.

I like to imagine at that Whitsun Fair
The gift of tongues was hovering in the air
Waiting to stoop
Headlong with equal triumph, Lee-ward bound,
To snatch him up into a field of sound
Laurelled and cock-a-hoop.

And when the pilgrimage is made,
The shadow meeting with the shade,
The graver music will be purling still
By Painswick stream and Birdlip Hill.

Laurie, wearing a coat of confidence, which came from walking out one midsummer morning to explore the world beyond the Slad Valley. He was nineteen, 'still soft at the edges', and with the need to cloak any apprehensions behind a cloud of cigarette smoke. He was heading for London, a hundred miles to the east, but because he had never seen the sea, he decided on a slight detour – via Southampton! It took him a week to reach the coast and experience his first sea breeze. The South Coast, however, never lived up to the promise of Thomas Hardy and he was soon heading for the capital, recording his first sight of it as 'a long smoky skyline hazed by the morning sun and filling the whole of the eastern horizon'.

In addition to the tributes of Laurie's peers, we also have the master's own words to help us build bulwarks against ordinariness. I know it isn't an easy task for anyone else to match Laurie's dulcet tones, especially that wonderful Gloucestershire burr, and I know – from many a contretemps with him on the subject – there are many very distinguished actors who have failed to meet the Lee test for speaking his words with feeling and understanding.

'He emotes in all the wrong ruddy places,' he once complained about a much-lauded Thespian I had booked for a BBC programme.

I was hesitant, therefore, about inviting anyone to read his material but I know Laurie would have approved of our choice of William Gaunt, an actor Laurie very much admired. Bill has never fallen into the trap of attempting the Cotswold accent but, instead, he endows Laurie's words with a ringing clarity.

My Many-Coated Man

Under the scarlet-licking leaves,
through bloody thought and bubbly shade,
the padded, spicy tiger moves –
a sheath of swords, a hooded blade.

The turtle on the naked sand
peels to the air his pewter snout
and rubs the sky with slotted shell –
the heart's dismay turned inside out.

The rank red fox goes forth at night
to bite the gosling's downy throat,
then digs his grave with panic claws
to share oblivion with the stoat.

The mottled moth, pinned to a tree,
woos with his wings the bark's disease
and strikes a fungoid, fevered pose
to live forgotten and at ease.

Like these, my many-coated man
shields his hot hunger from the wind,
and, hooded by a smile, commits
his private murder in the mind.

9

Laurie's 'My Many-Coated Man' provides us with the perfect theme for this remembrance and celebration of our poet because no one wore more coats more comfortably than Laurie Lee.

First and foremost, he enveloped himself in that warm, all-embracing coat of the husband and the father. This was his favourite garment, and it was worn with such a ferocious protectiveness that its sturdy fabric was seldom, if ever, breached by any of life's storms.

Today, Jessy and Cathy, who enclosed his later life as he himself put it, 'in a double embrace, like bookends', share their memories of Laurie with us and they have allowed me to metaphorically plunder his wardrobe in an exploration of the many facets of his more public persona.

All the world knew Laurie as a perceptive poet and a remarkable writer. Those of us lucky enough to have been a little closer also knew him as an accomplished musician and a maestro with the camera. He had more talents than any man is entitled to, a creativity that never allowed him to be still and had him changing coats at an astonishing rate.

He was also, for example, a wit, a traveller, a dedicated club-man and, oddly when you remember his passion for village life in Slad, he was something of a man-about-town. He was always excited to be at the centre of things in London. Here, around the Chelsea Arts Club, the Garrick, the Queen's Elm and sundry other watering holes, he revelled in the intellectual and social stimulus the city and its citizens afforded him.

As you will gather, Laurie's was a crowded cloakroom – impossibly crowded – so that a single person could not, with any certainty, sort out his many coats, or how or why he chose when and where to wear each of them.

With the help of his family and friends, we can only approach the problem with an idiosyncrasy that was so much of Laurie's nature. He enjoyed spontaneity above all else. He never knew boredom, because he shrugged it off instantly it appeared at his shoulder.

On the assumption that he has found a comfortable vantage-point on high and is looking down on us now – and no doubt taking child-like delight in the difficulty we're having pinning down his personality – let us each remember our many coated-man.

Perhaps the literary colleague who knew Laurie best, certainly longest, was John Mortimer. They first met at, of all places, the wartime Ministry of Information, where Laurie, unfit for the armed forces, was a caption-writer.

JOHN MORTIMER

Dear Laurie: I know from what you said – only, it seems, a little while ago – how much you regretted the incident that I am about to describe.

We have to go back over many years, more than half a century, to Pinewood Studios during the war. They were full of propaganda film units from the army, the navy and the air force with directors like the Boultings and Michael Powell and Carol Reed, and you were the scriptwriter of the Crown Film Unit making films for the Ministry of Information.

When I arrived, an amazingly thin, extremely nervous fourth assistant director, I caught sight of you from time to time. You were a poet I greatly admired, a small, attractive, bright-eyed figure playing a violin in a corridor and occasionally playing a flute.

You were clearly wishing you were back in Spain, walking through the dusty vineyards meeting dark-eyed señoritas, engaged in a war that seemed far more exciting than the drab task of fire-watching on the roof of Pinewood Studios.

As for me, I was a complete disaster. I'd taken the job as a young, serial film-fan who thought being an assistant director was an extraordinary, exciting and glamorous job. I found to my dismay that all it meant was getting tea for the director and saying 'Quiet, please!' at the beginning of every show. And being very nervous and timid as I am today, when I did call for quiet, everybody went on sawing wood and shouting and playing pontoon and making loud noises, and took not a blind bit of notice.

One day I lost my temper and yelled: 'Quiet, you bastards!' They all went on strike.

So I was taken aside and told that as I was one of the worst fourth assistant directors they had ever had, I would do far less harm if I was the scriptwriter.

You wanted to leave, anyway, so you said I could do it and I could have your job, provided I passed a test.

The test was to write a script about Watford Junction, and I went there on a bicycle and came back with some terrible script. I know perfectly well that you would have said it was wonderful whatever happened because you wanted to leave.

You did, very kindly, say it was wonderful. I was put in a uniform that had SCRIPTWRITER written on it, and that was the beginning of my writing career!

Over the years, however, you said again and again that you wished to God you had never sent me to Watford Junction because you were so irritated by these books that kept coming out . . .

And so we became friends. You were funny and ironic and friendly and kind-hearted, always.

We drank together when they had any beer in the Crooked Billet at Pinewood and we fell in love with the same girl, a soft-eyed, dark-haired beauty called Mavis. I hope she remembers us both with affection.

I knew how you hated to start writing. You would do anything rather than put pen to paper. You even reduced yourself to copying out the shipping news at the back of *The Times* to put off that evil moment.

But when you started, you wrote prose that was truly poetry and poetry that was beautiful in its simplicity.

I've been writing a film script of *Cider with Rosie* and I've got to know you and the book so well, and I hope I can do it justice.

It is far from a soft, rustic idyll. It is much concerned with death and poverty and some madness, the toughness as well as the sweetness of life close to Nature.

Like all good writers, like all good people, you never lost touch with your childhood but remembered it entirely without sentimentality. There is a passage – in which you write about the essential sanity, the quiet tolerance of village life, of country life – that is worth remembering at a time when the young seem to fill us full of fear and disapproval.

Sooner or later one was always caught out, but the thing was as readily forgotten; very little in the village was either secret or shocking, we merely repeated ourselves. Such early sex-games were formal exercises, a hornless charging of calves; but we were certainly lucky to live in a village, the landscape abounded with natural instruction which we imitated as best we could; if anyone saw us they laughed their heads off – and there were no magistrates to define us obscene. . .

As for us boys, it is certain that most of us, at some stage or other of our growth, would have been rounded up under present law, and quite a few shoved into reform school. Instead we emerged – culpable it's true – but unclassified in criminal record. No wilder or milder than Battersea boys, we were less ensnared by by-laws. If caught in the act, we got a quick bashing; and the fists of the farmer we'd robbed of apples or eggs seemed more natural and just than any cold-mouthed copper adding one more statistic for the book.

Dear Laurie: you thought about death and wrote a lot about it, but your writing is immortal and generation after generation will be the happier, the wiser and the better for reading it.

After the rigours of walking through Spain and suffering some of the nightmares of the Civil War, Laurie gladly donned the more comfortable coat of the poet-about-town. He settled back in London, more determined than ever to pursue a career as a writer, but knowing that a snatch of music would bring back the memories of his astonishing experience. He had gone to Spain with his violin and a repertoire of family favourites – 'Loch Lomond', 'The Rose of Tralee' and sundry other ballads – but returned able to conjure up the fire and passion of the flamenco and *paso doble* on the guitar.

With his literary success, Laurie found a second home – or was it third or fourth home? – at the Chelsea Arts Club. Here, improbably for a yokel son of the Cotswolds, he was always at ease, bantering with the snooker-playing metropolitan regulars, joking about the naked truth revealed by the latest cosmopolitan nude to be hung in the club-room, and proudly glorying in his life (and therefore honorary) membership.

He wore his club-man's coat with style and clearly found great comfort in the camaraderie it guaranteed. While he adored the flamboyance of the Garrick Club's salmon-and-cucumber tie and the many theatrical links it helped forge, he always regarded Chelsea as the next best thing to Slad.

Just round the corner from his metaphoric London garret, the Arts Club allowed him to revel in the company of fellow poets, including Roger McGough.

ROGER McGOUGH

I was in my early fifties when a daughter happened to me and, she being my first daughter, I felt a mixture of exhilaration and panic, and it was in Laurie that I confided. I knew that he'd been down the road himself and he was very encouraging to me, offering both wit and wisdom.

I remember him saying: 'Roger, don't worry! Just relax and enjoy it. Before you know where you are, she'll be borrowing money from you.'

Of course, he was right – almost.

Isabel is now seven but I'm borrowing money from her!

Here is a poem, a very short poem, I wrote for Laurie on his eightieth birthday. It's called 'All for Laurie Lee':

> I love the way he uses words
>   Will they work as well for me?
> 'Sorry,' said the words,
>   'We only do it for Laurie Lee.'

But words are common property
   They're available and free
Said the words: 'We're very choosy
   And we've chosen Laurie Lee.'

I want to write like he does
   But the words did all agree:
'Sorry son we're spoken for,
   We belong to Laurie Lee!'

The second 'reading' in this celebration of one of England's most remarkable, romantic writers is taken from Chapter 12 of the book of Laurie, Cider with Rosie:

Never to be forgotten, that first long secret drink of golden fire, juice of those valleys and of that time, wine of wild orchards, of russet summer, of plump red apples, and Rosie's burning cheeks. Never to be forgotten, or ever tasted again. . .

I put down the jar with a gulp and a gasp. Then I turned to look at Rosie. She was yellow and dusty with buttercups and seemed to be purring in the gloom; her hair was rich as a wild bee's nest and her eyes were full of stings. I did not know what to do about her, nor did I know what not to do. She looked smooth and precious, a thing of unplumbable mysteries, and perilous as quicksand.

'Rosie . . .' I said, on my knees, and shaking.

She crawled with a rustle of grass towards me, quick

and superbly assured. Her hand in mine was like a small wet flame which I could neither hold nor throw away. Then Rosie, with a remorseless, reedy strength, pulled me down from my tottering perch, pulled me down, down into her wide green smile and into the deep sub-aqueous grass.

Then I remember little, and that little, vaguely. Skin drums beat in my head. Rosie was close-up, salty, an invisible touch, too near to be seen or measured. And it seemed that the wagon under which we lay went floating away like a barge, out over the valley where we rocked unseen, swinging on motionless tides.

Then she took off her boots and stuffed them with flowers. She did the same with mine. Her parched voice crackled like flames in my ears. More fires were started. I drank more cider. Rosie told me outrageous fantasies. She liked me, she said, better than Walt, or Ken, Boney Harris, or even the curate. And I admitted to her, in a loud, rough voice, that she was even prettier than Betty Gleed. For a long time, we sat with our mouths very close, breathing the same hot air. We kissed, once only, so dry and shy, it was like two leaves colliding in air.

At last the cuckoos stopped singing and slid into the woods. The mowers went home and left us. I heard Jack calling as he went down the lane, calling my name till I heard him no more. And still we lay in our wagon of grass tugging at each other's hands, while her husky, perilous whisper drugged me and the cider beat gongs in my head. . .

Those gongs never did stop beating in Laurie's head. I suspect many friends will have their own story about Laurie's appreciation of the opposite sex: he himself revelled in stories that illustrate the impact he had on women of all ages over many years.

Even when the calendar said he should have been past it, Laurie delighted in flirtation and . . . I suspect even now, wherever he may be, he is still sipping enthusiastically from the cider flagon!

But this gentle flightiness detracted nothing from Laurie's enduring love for Two Women. *In the André Deutsch book by that title, Laurie pays his own tribute – in words and pictures – to his wife, Cathy, and his daughter, Jessy, both fixed within his rural idyll, Slad, where he had finally taken Cathy after twelve years in London.*

We moved in in the autumn, and I returned to boyhood, gathering and cutting wood.

The Victorian range soon crackled with beech-twigs and pine-cones, and washing steamed in front of it as in the days of my Mother. Cathy began to clear the garden. She burnt old leaves and wore a special hat. She seemed to be making a nest, but she also stood for long minutes at a time just gazing at the ground or out across the valley.

I think I remember her most clearly, during those first days at the cottage, as someone who felt herself locked out, a wistful fugitive, peering in through the windows as though seeking to be admitted; eyes large and questioning, still wondering who she was, where and to whom she most truly belonged.

True, we'd been married twelve years now, boxed-up in sterile London, with her ripe golden self still inexplicably childless. Now I'd brought her back to my beginnings, to the place where I was born and formed, a re-starting and starting ground for us both.

When it happened, by what magic did it come about? What spell had been preserved here for us? Was it the angle of the light, the special dew in the stones, the local pitch of birdsong, the close thrust of the hills? What was it, after twelve years, that finally loosed the knot, set the seed, and worked the miracle?

I still don't know. But one morning I walked into the kitchen and found Cathy perched up on the window-sill. She looked at me transfigured, her eyes full of confusion and triumph.

'Oh, Lol!' she said. 'Would you believe it? . . . I'm pregnant.' And she slipped into my arms and wept.

More tears of joy were shed, by Laurie this time, when he welcomed his new daughter to Slad to, of course, the music of Schubert, hoping he said, 'that such deep beauty and calm might be absorbed by the child'.

Jessy we called her, and she grew quickly from her first bruised softness to a sturdy, curly-haired beauty, a Pears'-soap angel with a sharp sting of carbolic, a thing of surging and unknowable forces. Had Cathy, in the long stillness and abstraction of her twelve married years, known she had been waiting for this? For all the first overcoatings of sentimental expectations, Jessy soon proved to be a paint-stripping reality, and Cathy welcomed and embraced her like a demon lover.

As she grew and changed, I was increasingly wondering what this new girl could be, with her ecstatic adorations and rages. The beaming knife-keen awakening, cracking the dawn like an egg, her furies at the small frets of living, the long fat slumbers, almost continental in their reaches, the bedtimes of chuckles, private jokes and languors.

And who was I to her? The rough dark shadow of pummelling games and shouts, the cosy frightener, the tossing and swinging arms, lifting the body to the highest point of hysteria before lowering it back again to the safe male smell.

But she was my girl now, the second force in my life,

and with her puffed, knowing eyes, forever moving with colour and light, she was well aware of it.

Cathy and Jessy made a devastating combination. They entranced Laurie, and looking at the beautiful photographs of them, it is easy to understand his passion. His adoration never faded.

Mother and daughter, nearer together now and more alike than they know, have balanced the greater part of my recent years. Easy to love such clamouring, hungry and beautiful assailants; not so easy to remain unscathed. By crowding my days and stealing my sleep, they have also lengthened my life.

All love lives by slowly moving towards its end, and is sharpened by the snake-bite of farewell within it. The birth of my child was a farewell to the child-bride who bore her. And my daughter, now grown, must be another farewell. Perhaps I have lost both of them now, as time withdraws them from me.

Laurie worried unnecessarily: time has not – nor could not – cause his two favourite women to withdraw. There is no perhaps: they are far from lost to him. Nor, while they have his favourite music in their lives, will he be lost to them. Bobby Kok describes Laurie's musician's coat.

BOBBY KOK

I met Laurie when I moved to the Slad Valley and when I found we shared a love of music, music-making and Gloucestershire. When I heard him play the violin, I also realized that his playing matched the quality I had found in his writings. We play this slow movement in the belief that Laurie would have shared with us the eternal, seraphic quality of the music.

[Mr Kok and colleagues from the Chamber Orchestra of London then played the slow movement from Haydn's Quartet in D major, Opus 76, No. 5.]

If Laurie hadn't been a writer, he would almost certainly have worn his musician's coat full time. He loved listening to music and constantly used Schubert to still his restless mind. He was even more enthusiastic about playing and especially loved the impact the rhythms of the Spanish guitar had on listeners. He had many professional musicians amongst his friends and they constantly pressed him to join the concert circuit. As it was, he settled for a small, but discerning audience – in this instance, wife Cathy and daughter Jessy – for his throbbing guitar solos.

❦ Allow me just for one brief moment to be prosaic, to step outside the metaphor, to talk about a real *coat. Laurie had, for most of his early life, just one coat (indeed, for a fair bit of it he didn't even have a coat at all). But, almost as a symbol of his success, he acquired his famous army officer's topcoat. His British Warm, he called it, and he used it – through its several editions – to fend off the world. Behind this coat he concealed his own uncertainties, and he also used it to restrain a natural flamboyance which always surprised him and sometimes even embarrassed him.*

His role as a poet and writer, he insisted, was to observe, *not to* be *observed. He reasoned that no one seeing the comfortable, unpretentious greatcoat would look beyond the outer wrapping: leaving the inner man to wander the world in peace absorbing cameos of other people's lives.*

When he wasn't hiding behind his coat, Laurie often enveloped himself in a cloak of secrecy, much of it surrounding the battered briefcase he seemed to grow on the end of his arm. No reflection of his latter years could ignore the secrets it contained though it's true to say that some of these were less secret than others.

The greatest secret involved the manuscript he carried in it for at least twenty years to my knowledge. While many of us knew it was there, no one could prise from him any information about its subject-matter nor even whether it was complete or still in the course of being written.

The briefcase seldom left his side. He used it as a tease to the London publishing world, as a defence against those who tried to cajole him into greater productivity and, as it transpired, as a form of creative life insurance. He was fearful that publication would be his literary swansong, and he reckoned, therefore, that the longer the manuscript stayed in his briefcase, the longer would his creativity continue.

We now know, of course, that the manuscript was the third element of his biography, A Moment of War, *which he finally gave up – in 1991 – to the care of Penguin's publishing director, Tony Lacey.*

TONY LACEY

I am sure there are many people in the congregation who knew Laurie a great deal longer and a great deal better than I did, so it's a rather humbling and somewhat frightening experience to be talking about him in such a public way.

But I would like to think that it is justified for two reasons, beyond the obvious one that I liked the man and admired his talents so much.

First, in some sense I represent a relationship that Laurie had with his publishers, Penguin, for thirty-five years: *Cider with Rosie* was first published in paperback in 1962 and has never been out of print since that day – despite what Laurie would sometimes mischievously claim to believe.

'I suppose you'll be letting it go, then,' he would say to me occasionally on the telephone on a dismal Monday afternoon. This, of one of our best-selling titles which we had no conceivable reason to let go out of print.

The relationship was not an abstract one, although I do think he rather liked to be in this most famous of all imprints. His pleasure was palpable when we told him not long before he died that we planned to do an edition of the book in our Twentieth-Century Classics series.

But really his relationship was with people, people doing very many different kinds of jobs in the house, and it's absolutely significant that so many of them, of different generations, are here in St James's: chairmen, editors-in-chief, publishing directors, art directors, people who sold his books, people who marketed his books and people who paid his royalties – a department that Laurie would probably deny had ever existed!

Because the truth was that, though I like to think – no, I know – he liked very many of us as individuals, in some ways he didn't have much time for publishers. He can't possibly have really believed all those tales he would tell me during those long, wonderful afternoons at the Chelsea Arts Club about the terrible experiences he had had over the years, with Penguin as with all the rest, but the attitude was clear.

I suppose I should have been offended but, in fact, his views rather suited my own temperament. Laurie may have believed that God's house is one of many mansions but, if so, he surely believed that publishers occupied the grubby basement while the truly creative people had the very best, sunshine-filled rooms. Laurie loved poets and painters and musicians, and who's a publisher to argue with that?

The second reason I am here is because I had the great good fortune to publish Laurie's last book, *A Moment of War*.

He had been telling us for some time that he'd finished a

book but, I'm sorry to say, there had come a time when I had stopped believing him. He wouldn't show me any of it, he wouldn't tell me what it was about, he wasn't even sure he wanted it published at all.

Then on one remarkable night we stepped out into the street after – what shall I say? – a particularly convivial evening and he suddenly asked, 'Well, do you want to publish it? What's it worth?'

This was difficult to answer since I hadn't read a word, but I hazarded a somewhat inebriated, abstract guess, he seemed pleased and we shook hands.

A few days later a brown parcel arrived and in it, to my immense joy and no little relief, was what I truly believe to be a small masterpiece: the brilliant, spare, harsh book that is *A Moment of War*, surely the perfect answer to all those blind enough to find only nostalgia and loss in his books.

It was like the perfect winning goal scored in the last five minutes before the end of the game, that silences one half of the crowd and sends the other half home elated. I can't resist the metaphor since Laurie teased me pretty mercilessly about my passion for football on many occasions. He saw it, I fear, as another piece of publishers' vulgarity.

There's a small coda to this story. We didn't yet have a clear run because Laurie now insisted that the manuscript had to be read by a mysterious person whom he called his literary adviser. To this day I don't know who this person was, or indeed whether he or she really existed, but word finally came back that approval had been given and we could proceed to publication, though with no very great hope of success or acclaim.

Both came, of course, the minute the book was published.

The critics and the reading public recognized that after a very long wait, Laurie had written another wonderful book – and I truly believe he knew it too, which gives me a great deal of pleasure today.

The eyes have it – and reveal Mr Lee, ladies' man and wit. This is the Laurie Lee known and adored by his female friends, deliciously wicked in stringing along another young beauty, this one in the garden of the Chelsea Arts Club.

As Tony Lacey said, A Moment of War *evokes a very different mood from* Cider with Rosie *and* As I Walked Out One Midsummer Morning. *It's altogether darker, more intense, Laurie at his most profound and in the soldier's greatcoat.*

It tells of his role – a mere 'bit part', he insisted – in the Spanish Civil War and, in particular, it reflects his admiration of the bravery of the ordinary people of Spain.

The night was long and cramped as the train lumbered inland, slowly circling and climbing the escarpment of Chiclana to reach the freezing tableland of Mancha. I had known part of this plateau in the heat of high summer when it seemed to blaze and buckle like a copper sheet. Now it was as dead as the Russian steppes, an immensity of ashen snow reflecting the hard light of the winter moon. No gold path of glory, this, for youth to go to war, but a grey path of intense disquiet. . .

In a bitter dawn we approached Albacete on the plain, clanking through tiny stations where groups of snow-swept women watched us dumbly as we passed them by. A lad at a level crossing, with a thin, head-down horse, lifted a clenched fist for a moment, then dejectedly dropped it again. Silent old men and barefooted children, like Irish peasants of the Great Hunger, lined the sides of the tracks without gesture or greeting. We were received, as we trundled towards our military camp, not as heroic deliverers, or reinforcements for victory, but rather as another train-load of faceless prisoners seen through a squint-eyed blankness of spirit.

But as we steamed at last into Albacete station, we found that someone, at least, had dredged up some sense of occasion. We fell stiffly from the train and lined up raggedly on the platform, and were faced by a small brass band like a firing-squad. In the dead morning light they pointed their instruments at our heads and blew out a succession of tubercular blasts. Then a squat mackin-toshed Commander climbed on to a box and addressed us in rasping tones. Until that moment, perhaps, cold and hungry though we were, we may still have retained some small remnants of courage. The Commander took them away from us, one by one, and left us with nothing but numb dismay.

One man who knew Laurie, and knows the Spanish landscape and the Spanish people, is the Ambassador of Ireland to Spain, His Excellency Richard Ryan.

HIS EXCELLENCY RICHARD RYAN

I first met Laurie in 1965 with the poet Patrick Kavanagh and other literary luminaries in the Bailey pub in Dublin. Laurie was a famous poet and the celebrated author of *Cider with Rosie*. I was a mere poetry-struck teenager, mildly shocked and rather agape at the fast-flowing conversation, fuelled by fast-flowing Guinness and whiskey, as these literary giants conversed with much scholarship not about poetry, but the science of how to make an adequate living from backing racehorses.

During my long posting at our London Embassy in the 'eighties, on the run as I sometimes was from the not infrequent stresses of what we always described as the close Anglo-Irish inter-governmental relationship (close indeed, sometimes too close for comfort), I relished Laurie's exquisitely droll way of observing the world – whether from a corner of the Queen's Elm or of the Garrick Club bar, or half concealed behind a strategically situated bush in the Chelsea Arts Club garden, dipping occasionally into a brimming Scotch and its accompanying ale.

Among many memories, I cherish one of Laurie, *en route* to a black-tie dinner as my guest at the embassy, a most elegant figure in that cream linen jacket which he sported, having his salmon-and-cucumber Garrick Club bow-tie painstakingly affixed by an obliging policeman outside the Chelsea Arts Club, as the embassy car waited to convey him to Grosvenor Place.

Following my posting three years ago to our Madrid Embassy, Laurie and I began to plan what he called an extended farewell visit to Spain. While this was postponed by recurring eye trouble or the odd bit of flu, he discussed, in his punctilious way, at length and many times, the fine points of the route – by boat and train – that would bring him and Cathy, and perhaps Jessy too, to the country which he painted so vividly in three of his finest books, *As I Walked Out One Midsummer Morning*, *A Rose for Winter* and *A Moment of War*.

He decided that we would dine on cochinillo, suckling pig, and the fine wines of the Duero at the famous eighteenth-century restaurant, Mesón de Candido, in Segovia, where, sixty years before, having curled up for the night in his blanket under the great Roman aqueduct, he had in mid-morning pressed his nose against Candido's window-pane, tears of pure hunger on his cheeks as the baby pigs, apples in snouts, sent from the oven their remorselessly delicious flavours to his quivering nose outside.

He decided that we would take a copita or two, or three, in the Madrid bar Las Cuevas de Luis Candelas, where, he speculated, he might just recognize in the features of some pretty girl those of her mother, or perhaps grandmother, who once, like himself, could – and perhaps did – return a lingering glance over a vino tinto or a manzanilla.

We would, he decided, visit the Alhambra in Granada, a book in hand of the great Moorish poems lamenting its loss to the Christian fundamentalists; and we would walk to the caves above Granada in the foothills of the towering Sierra Nevada, where the gypsy girls danced for him and with him, their hair, as he put it so well, like a couple of pints of coal tar.

In our last long conversation, a month or so before he died, I told him how four of those gitanas, the gypsy women, had descended like huge crows on my wife and me and our boys, as we sat at a pavement café outside the Alcázar in Segovia. By the time I repelled them, I told Laurie crossly, my wallet and my wife's handbag had disappeared under their flying skirts. 'Dear boy,' said Laurie gently, 'don't be boring. Don't tell me about handbags. Tell me about their eyes, their teeth, their hair. Weren't they gorgeous?'

I had to admit that his was the wiser perspective on the matter and that, in their wild way, they were, indeed, gorgeous.

The richness, the diversity, the drama, above all perhaps the un-European extremes of Spain – described by Auden as 'that arid square, that fragment nipped off from hot Africa, soldered so crudely to inventive Europe' – have, over the centuries, drawn a stream of observers, commentators, artists and writers as diverse as Washington Irving, George Borrow, Friedrich Engels, Richard Ford, George Orwell, Walter Starkie, Ernest

Hemingway, Roy Campbell, Karl Marx, Gerald Brenan, Ian Gibson, and, among the most gifted of all, and perhaps the most treasured by us, Laurie Lee.

He was a fine poet and a very fine poet in prose. In his three Spanish books we have autobiographical writing of the highest order, with its essentially poetic patina overlaying always-steely observation, the instantly recognizable Laurie Lee touch. Along with his Gloucestershire masterpiece, *Cider with Rosie*, this writing has ensured Laurie a cherished place in the hearts of millions of readers around the world, including Spain, where he is much and widely loved. These three books contain some of the most memorable, truly observed encapsulations of a Spanish world which, like the rural England of his childhood, has passed away and left to us too few authentic traces.

But Laurie's vision was never a simple, sentimental smile-and-a-tear chronicle of the world (in James Joyce's image), of the lost 'dearly beloved'. In addition to unsentimental, crystal-clear recollection of the rural England of his childhood and the Spain of his early adulthood, always tinged with and controlled by a droll and ultimately distanced English eye, there is also, again and again in his writing, so much of the unchanging heart of Spain – the huge landscapes of Castilla, La Mancha and Andalucia, the violence of sunlight and contrasts of colour, the enigmatic character of the people, the extreme characteristics of the country adumbrated by Auden – that Laurie captures repeatedly with the absolute, immediate smack of authenticity.

Take, for example, what he can work in in a few words on a Madrid bar:

> . . . under the terracotta roofs, a proliferation of caves of ice. With carters, porters, watchmen, taxi-drivers, sleek dandies, and plump officials sipping their golden wines, fastidiously peeling a prawn, biting into the tart pink flesh of a lobster, tasting the living brine of half-forgotten seas, of half-remembered empires, while the surge of conversation continued like bubbling water under the framed pictures of bulls and heroes.

Writing like this makes you taste the sherry, the prawn, the place, the history.

He could enter Spain in this magic way and still the Englishman in him could recoil, sometimes just in time, when its narcotic Catholicism almost closed like water over him as it did over so many other visitors. In *A Rose for Winter*, his mostly gentle description of his return, with Cathy, to Andalucia, he was struck down by a fever and heard, as it were from a long way off, female discussion of arrangements for his own funeral and optimistic speculation as to how beautiful a widow Cathy would make:

'"Ay, Lorenzo . . . How lucky you are. Everybody is saying what a beautiful widow the señora will make. Even now the students make speeches to her. She will never want for a husband. Do not concern yourself about her."' A sudden rage consumed the man from Gloucestershire who sat bolt upright, in Lazarine fashion, to see Cathy already dressed in anticipatory black by the Spanish women.

' "Take that stuff off!" he cried. "And clear those bastards off the stairs!" ' There was silence, then stumbling as the suitors ran into the street. Laurie observed laconically in the next sentence which, I think, only an Englishman could write: 'From then on I improved rapidly.'

Laurie would have been an honoured guest in colleges and universities throughout Spain. Many distinguished cathedra-ticos from great Spanish universities, hearing that *el famoso* Lorenzo Lee might re-visit Spain, wanted him to honour their institutions by a no-matter-how-brief visit.

His single injunction regarding that last Spanish journey was, however, that we should avoid all encounters with aca-demics and officials, no matter how kindly their intentions.

Sadly, the visit was not to happen. We in Spain, like Laurie's admirers throughout the world, are saddened by his passing, although we celebrate the richness of his life and the enriching qualities which his great craftsmanship bestowed around him.

Spain is honoured that one of England's most distinguished writers of this century devoted so much of his writing life to that complex and enigmatic country.

We will not now take those copitas of manzanilla in Las Cuevas de Luis Candelas in Madrid, or the suckling pig and the powerful wines of the Duero in Segovia, or read Moorish poetry in the gardens of the Alhambra in Granada.

But I feel that Laurie presides now, from a little distance, over all these things because he touched them with his special way of seeing, of understanding, and that is his great, kindly gift to us.

Since his passing, as I travel through the Spain that, like Goya, he captured so authentically, I feel that he is strolling there too, a little way off – the familiar stocky figure with tousled hair, the mahogany complexion of late summer, perhaps the cream linen jacket and that sideways, quizzical look of his from under the ubiquitous Panama hat – and I think that he is chuckling quietly to himself, near us.

Laurie's idea of heaven was to sit in quiet contemplation over a pint at his local pub, the Woolpack. It was here he felt at his most secure, a stone's throw from his home and in the midst of the village people who made few demands on him and never invaded his privacy.

⚘ Had Laurie planned this memorial, I'm quite sure at this stage he would have insisted in getting out his violin to play us a piece of his favourite Spanish music. Well, thanks to his expertise with the tape recorder, Laurie can now do just that!

[We then played a piece of Spanish music recorded in 1942 – and in true Laurie style – on a Woolworth's cassette! Although the technical quality left something to be desired, the playing was brilliant.]

I had the job of adapting some of Laurie's writing for the radio. That was easy, because I could hear his voice in my head and I knew exactly what were the telling phrases. I also, of course, had to abridge some of his work and that was a nightmare: Laurie's writing is tight and economic, probably because he hated the labour of writing!

He was almost pathologically reluctant to don his writer's coat and always had a ready stock of excuses for not doing so.

He sharpened his famous, soft-black pencils . . . made tea . . . sharpened his pencils again . . . went for a walk . . . made more tea . . . and then sharpened the pencils yet again.

In truth, he painfully had to squeeze out every word and trap it on the page, and once he had it there in front of him, he studied it from every angle, turned it over again and again to be sure that it was precisely the right word.

Brian Patten, I'm sure, recognizes something of that routine.

BRIAN PATTEN

I recognize the bit about sharpening pencils, but as far as the *right* words go, I think Laurie had the monopoly on them. I think he often kept a lot of them in the plastic bags he used to carry around with him.

It is a big claim but I believe that, more than any other writer this century, Laurie's words captured the sense of absolute joy people can feel in their clearest moments towards the natural world. It is such an intense joy, and so fleeting, that to capture it in words is so really difficult and needs a touch of genius. I think that intensity is Laurie's great gift to us and also very much to the future.

The idea of him dying is to me absolutely absurd because I think Laurie will live as long as people actually read and actually listen to words. This poem of mine is called 'So Many Different Lengths of Time'. The first five lines are from the Spanish of Pablo Neruda and the rest is an answer to those five lines:

How long is a man's life, after all?
Is it a thousand days, or only one?
One week, or a few centuries?
How long does a man's death last?
And what do we mean when we say, 'gone forever'?

Adrift in such preoccupations, we seek clarification.
We can go to the philosophers,
But they will grow tired of our questions.
We can go to the priests and the rabbis
But they might be too busy with administrations.

* * *

So, how long does a man live, after all,
And how much does he live while he lives?
We fret, and ask so many questions –
Then when it comes to us
The answer is so simple.

A man lives for as long as we carry him inside us,
For as long as we carry the harvest of his dreams,
For as long as we ourselves live,
Holding memories in common, a man lives.

His wife will carry his man's scent, his touch;
His child will carry the weight of his love.
One friend will carry his arguments,
Another will hum his favourite tunes,
Another will still share his terrors.

And the days will pass with baffled faces,
Then the weeks, then the months,
Then there will be a day when no question is asked,
And the knots of grief will loosen in the stomach,
And the puffed faces will calm.
And on that day he will not have ceased,
But will have ceased to be separated by death.
How long does a man live, after all?

A man lives so many different lengths of time.

Among the millions who read Laurie's books are the GCSE students presented with Cider with Rosie *as a set book. He didn't wear the educationalist's coat any lighter than he did the writer's. He knew this was an astonishing compliment to his writing, but his insecurities left him feeling it was a dubious honour. He was afraid that being forced to read him at school might put them off reading him – or, even worse, from actually buying his books! – when they grew up.*

The Secretary of State for Education and Employment, the Right Honourable David Blunkett, MP, knows better.

Laurie the educationist, rubbing shoulders with a future Secretary of State for Education. Before Labour won the 1997 General Election, the Rt Hon. David Blunkett, MP visited Slad to talk to Laurie for a special edition of BBC Radio 4's *Down Your Way*. After posing for this archive photograph, Mr Blunkett remembers going into the Woolpack and succumbing to a subconscious urge to drink cider.

RT HON. DAVID BLUNKETT, MP

I first got to know Laurie and Cathy when I visited their home in Slad, as the interviewer rather than the interviewee, for BBC Radio 4's *Down Your Way*. At lunchtime, when we went across to the Woolpack, I found myself almost inadvertently asking for a glass of cider.

Some books are about poetry. Some of them are about prose. But Laurie's books are poetry and prose, enabling me to see the environment in which he lived, enabling all of us to see the picture of people, of families and, of course, of the moment in history that he was describing.

Cider with Rosie was a book for all times and a book for all generations, and I take pleasure in those passages about his school-days.

> Our village school was poor and crowded, but in the end I relished it. It had a lively reek of steaming life: boys' boots, girls' hair, stoves and sweat, blue ink, white chalk, and shavings.

Not exactly New Labour, I have to say, and yet Laurie's desire
for people to be able to read, to spell, to do their tables, is
reflected in what he wrote:

> . . . we rocked to our chanting, hammering the gold nails
> home.

And *we're* doing that today. By way of a social observation,
there was no one who had greater perception of welfare without soul.

Laurie's description of the Browns is, in my view, unmatched
anywhere. He said Joseph and Hannah Brown appeared to be
indestructible:

> For as long as I could remember they had lived together
> in the same house by the common. They had lived there,
> it was said, for fifty years; which seemed to me for ever.
> They had raised a large family and sent them out into the
> world, and had continued to live on alone, with nothing
> left of their noisy brood save some dog-eared letters and
> photographs.
>
> The old couple were as absorbed in themselves as
> lovers, content and self-contained; they never left the
> village or each other's company, they lived as snug as
> two podded chestnuts. By day blue smoke curled up from
> their chimney, at night the red windows glowed; the

cottage, when we passed it, said 'Here live the Browns,' as though that were part of nature.

And then he describes what happened to the Browns.

. . . suddenly, within the space of two days, feebleness took them both. It was as though two machines, wound up and synchronized, had run down at exactly the same time . . .

Well, the Authorities were told; the Visiting Spinsters got busy; and it was decided they would have to be moved. They were too frail to help each other now, and their children were too scattered, too busy. There was but one thing to be done; it was for the best; they would have to be moved to the Workhouse.

The old couple were shocked and terrified, and lay clutching each other's hands. 'The Workhouse' – always a word of shame, grey shadow falling on the close of life, most feared by the old (even when called The Infirmary); abhorred more than debt, prison, or beggary, or even the stain of madness.

Hannah and Joseph thanked the Visiting Spinsters but pleaded to be left at home, to be left as they wanted, to cause no trouble, just simply to stay together.

But the spinsters insisted:

'You'll be well looked after,' the Spinsters said, 'and you'll see each other twice a week.' The bright busy voices cajoled with authority and the old couple were not trained to defy them. So that same afternoon, white and speechless, they were taken away to the Workhouse. Hannah Brown was put to bed in the Women's Wing, and Joseph lay in the Men's. It was the first time, in all their fifty years, that they had ever been separated. They did not see each other again, for in a week they both were dead.

Laurie speaks of this having haunted him like no other death and reflects sadly on what he calls 'the kind, killing Authority' that arranged it.

And *I* celebrate Laurie Lee because, in enabling people to enjoy reading and learning, in enabling people to see the world as it is and to challenge the bright authority of those spinsters all those years ago, Laurie enables us to stop the 'killing kindness' and to ensure that we have a world that celebrates joy.

Squire Lee, country gentleman. Refusing to acknowledge the years, and shrugging off the failing eyesight that forced him to use a white stick, Laurie bestrode his Cotswold parish, master of all he surveyed. In *Cider with Rosie*, he said he didn't know where he was born, but that never bothered him because he always insisted his life effectively began when the family settled in Slad. Certainly, that is where he regarded as 'home'.

Having walked the wanderlust out of his soul, he eventually took his young wife back there in the 1960s and from then on he always tried to be in his house, next to the Woolpack, so he could enjoy the rising of each full moon over Painswick Hill.

We are now firmly back in Slad, where Laurie was born and where, with a little help from his beloved mother, his creativity first took flight and resulted in Cider with Rosie.

Time squared itself, and the village shrank, and distances crept nearer. The sun and moon, which once rose from our hill, rose from London now in the east. One's body was no longer a punching ball, to be thrown against trees and banks, but a telescoping totem crying strange demands few of which we could yet supply. In the faces of the villagers one could see one's change, and in their habits their own change also. The horses had died; few people kept pigs any more but spent their spare time buried in engines. The flutes and cornets, the gramophones with horns, the wind harps were thrown away – now wireless aerials searched the electric sky for the music of the Savoy Orpheans. Old men in the pubs sang, 'As I Walked Out', then walked out and never came back. Our Mother was grey now, and a shade more lightheaded, talking of mansions she would never build.

As for me – for me, the grass grew longer, and more sorrowful, and the trees were surfaced like flesh, and girls were no longer to be treated lightly but were creatures of commanding sadness, and all journeys through the valley were now made alone, with passion in every bush, and the motions of wind and cloud and stars were suddenly for myself alone, and voices elected me of all men living and called me to deliver the world, and I groaned from solitude, blushed when I stumbled, loved strangers and bread and butter, and made long trips through the rain on my bicycle, stared wretchedly through lighted windows, grinned wryly to think how little I was known, and lived in a state of raging excitement.

The sisters, as I said, were about to get married. Harold was working at a factory lathe. Brother Jack was at Grammar School, and his grammar was excellent; and Tony still had a fine treble voice. My Mother half-knew me, but could not help, I felt doomed, and of all things wonderful.

It was then that I began to sit on my bed and stare out at the nibbling squirrels, and to make up poems from intense abstraction, hour after unmarked hour, imagination scarcely faltering once, rhythm hardly skipping a beat, while sisters called me, suns rose and fell, and the poems I made, which I never remembered, were the first and last of that time . . .

It's fitting, I think, that the final word in this celebration of our many-coated man should come from Gloucestershire. It was there Laurie found first the encouragement of his family, and then the inspiration of the landscape and the people who lived in that small, tight-knit community of Slad – just one mile long and a mile and a half wide.

From there, Laurie's neighbour, fellow writer and, most importantly, close friend, P. J. Kavanagh, brings his tribute.

66

P. J. KAVANAGH

Let us reflect on the hymn with which this memorial service began, 'Now thank we all our god with heart and hands and voices'. That's something that Laurie did. The extraordinary thing about Laurie's prose – his poetry is another matter: it's much more grave – was that he used it to celebrate his experience of living.

Every experience seemed new-born. In other words it was youthful, and he retained this youth for a blessedly long time, far into middle age.

But the ageing of a person like Laurie is particularly painful because you're losing not only your strength, but also, perhaps, your wits. You are losing your stock-in-trade, losing what you have to offer the world.

Laurie, of course, replaced this by something very remarkable and I had an opportunity to watch this happening gradually over forty years, both as a neighbour in London and as a neighbour in Gloucestershire. He replaced it with a particular quality of attention to other people, particularly when talking one to one.

He's been called flirtatious and there was that quality about him. He wanted to make people like him but, far more importantly, as I watched I saw what he was doing: he was giving to others a greater affection for themselves. He always sent people away feeling better about themselves and he put enormous energy into that.

We had a celebration of Laurie at the Cheltenham Literary Festival and I mentioned this on stage, and in the interval between the events that followed I was hanging about and an extraordinary number of people came up and said, 'Yes, that happened. Yes, he came and spoke to me and I felt marvellous.' These were, so to speak, ordinary people, not famous people.

I remember Laurie once saying to me indignantly about a certain contemporary poet: 'All his friends are called Stravinsky or Winston or Isaiah. He doesn't seem to have any friends called Joe Bloggs.' The thing about Laurie was that he never ever forgot Joe Bloggs and that is why Joe Bloggs loved Laurie.

But he was also a man of indignation. He contained *savoir indignasio* at what we do to the world, the world in London as well as the world in Gloucestershire because, as it's been said, he was very much a Londoner. He didn't wear string around the bottom of his trousers.

One of my favourite pieces of Laurie's poetry illustrates clearly how economic he could be in his writing. This is a little poem he put, presumably, at the end of his *Selected Poems* and he must have valued it and I value it as I value his poetry a great deal, and it's called 'The Pollard Beech' and it refers to that extraordinary brutality with which, sometimes, we treat London trees – cutting them to the quick.

> Blue-pencil knife, to keep it brief,
> Edits the sprawled loquacious beech,
> And clips each hyperbolic leaf
> To fit the city's stumpy speech.
>
> Till, like a slogan, trim and terse,
> It stands and sums up in a word
> The gist of that once epic verse
> Whose every branch rhymed with a bird.

This picturesque churchyard was always going to be Laurie's last resting-place. Dramatically poised above the lush, green Slad Valley, he reckoned he would spend eternity pondering life's great mysteries 'secure under a bit of nice Cotswold stone that will protect me from the damned Welsh rain'.